The Elite
of the Fleet
Volume 1

A guide to the embroidered emblems
worn by naval aviators - 1927 to present

J. L. Pete Morgan

The Elite of the Fleet Vol. 1

Author, J. L. Pete Morgan
Copyright © 1990
All rights reserved. Except for use in a review, no portion of this book may be reproduced in any form without the express written permission of the publisher.

Library of Congress catalogue card number 90-081998
ISBN 0-9626310-0

Published by
International Trade Association
5914 E. Cactus Wren Road
Paradise Valley, AZ 85253
USA

Printed in Singapore

0 9 8 7 6 5 4 3 2 1

Design: Smit Ghormely Sanft

Photographer: Shane Morgan

The author wishes to extend heartfelt thanks to the following individuals for their gracious assistance and generous support in this project.

John C. McPherson • Lancer Militaria

Kent Spalding • K & S Militaria

Marty Rosholt • International Insignia, Inc.

Richard Rizzo • Squadron Flight Shop

Doug Barnard • Troutdale Aerodrome

Mel Hagan • San Francisco, CA

Wayne Hatley • TASC

Shane Morgan • Photographer

Frank Kruger • Military Bits & Pieces

Senator John McCain

Walt Taggert • USMC

J.G. "Dutch" Snow • Aero Art

The following organizations have been extremely helpful and cooperative in the production of this book.

McDonnell Douglas Aircraft Company

Grumman Aircraft Company

Northrup Aviation

Rockwell Aerospace

U.S. Navy

U.S. Marine Corps

And above all, to the lady without whose support none of this would have been possible. She has also become quite an authority on insignia and marketing in her own right... Sara Sue Morgan. My sincere thanks for your love, support and friendship through all this.

Table of Contents

Foreword

Himself a former naval aviator, John S. McCain is a 1958 graduate of the Naval Academy. On active duty, he flew with VA-46 *Clansmen* and VA-65 *Tigers*. During the Vietnam Conflict, he was shot down and spent 5½ years as a POW in North Vietnam. He retired with the rank of Captain USN and is currently United States Senator from Arizona. The Senator, his wife Cindy, and their children reside in Phoenix.

JOHN McCAIN
UNITED STATES SENATOR
WASHINGTON, DC 20510

In August, 1940 Winston Churchill said to the House of Commons, "Never in the field of human conflict was so much owed by so many to so few." He was, of course, referring to the spectacular courage displayed by Royal Air Force pilots in the Battle of Britain.

While England struggled valiantly for its survival, air components of the United States Navy, Marine Corps and Army were sharpening the skills that would serve us so well once we entered the war. The Mitchells and Doolittles were championing the cause of aviation as the next tactical breakthrough on the modern battlefield. The Battle of Britain reinforced their arguments and helped clear the way for the development of unequaled American air power.

It was the Navy, however, that first grasped the growing importance of air power to our national security. In a news release issued in 1914, "The Secretary of the Navy decided that the science of aerial navigation has reached that point where aircraft must form a large part of our naval forces for offensive and defensive operations."

Since that time, naval aviators and many battles that have tested their courage and skill have become legendary. In this book, The Elite of the Fleet, Pete Morgan provides us with a useful, well-documented history as well as a reference guide for naval aviation tradition. His work instructs us that the emblems worn by naval aviators bear a distinctiveness that reflects the type of aircraft flown and the pilot's unit designation.

The emblems and patches worn by naval pilots and crews are an enormous source of unit pride. Indeed, they were designed to evoke that pride. Unit camaraderie and cohesion were felt by every pilot and crewman who observed the unit colors proudly displayed on the tail of an A-4 or sewn to his well-worn flight jacket.

Pete Morgan's contribution to this proud tradition is to be applauded. His work adds to the legend of courage and dedication by which we have come to know the heroes of naval aviation.

John McCain

John McCain
United States Senator

This is planned to be the first of several books showing the insignia of US Naval Aviation. The scope of this first volume is to give an overall view of the subject. It is not intended to be the final authority on all related matters. It is beyond the scope of this book to begin with the histories of individual units or ships. That will be left to more scholarly publications. My purpose is to bring you some of the color, heraldry and pageantry associated with the insignia of Naval Aviation.

From its earliest beginnings on the first aircraft carrier, USS Langley, in 1922 to today's modern, nuclear powered, floating flying fields, the history of Naval Aviation has been one of proud and honorable tradition. Through the years, much of this tradition has been displayed on the uniforms, flight suits and the off-duty dress of the people associated with this arm of the naval service. I don't believe that, back in the 1920's, when VF-14 *Tophatters* first designed their patch, that they were aware of the custom they were creating and the ramifications it would hold in the future.

With the advent of World War II and the accompanying expansion of the naval air forces, the use of insignia became widespread as both a means of identification and for morale purposes. Today, every unit in the service must have its individual insignia or colors to guide upon.

Each member of a unit who call them-selves *Wildcats* or *Gladiators* or some name that indicates strength to themselves and defeat to the enemy feels more a part of the grand scheme of the ultimate goal of the military service. This feeling of pride or "esprit de corps" has always been of paramount importance in raising the level of performance and partici-pation in combat situations when an individuals sense of preservation is trying to dictate otherwise. This is precisely why sports teams have a great cheering section. The need to have a good feeling of pride can-not be overemphasized. The same is true with the use of insignia in the military. It gives the individual a sense of belonging to the team and pres-sure to do a job well so as not to let the team down.

So, to those intrepid aviators, who have never let the team down, this book is respectfully dedicated...

Fighter
Squadrons

Fighter
Squadrons

Fighter Squadrons

1. VF-1 Wolfpack

2. VF-1 Wolfpack

3. VF-1 Wolfpack

4. VF-1 "Movie Version" (also VAW-110)

5. VF-2 Bounty Hunters

6. VF-9A Fighting 9-A

7. VF-11 Red Rippers

8. VF-11 Red Rippers

9. VF-14 Tophatters

1

2

3

4

5

6

7

8

9

1

2

3

4

5

6

7

8

9

1. VF-45 — 4 and 20
2. VF-51
3. BE-DEVILERS
4. FIGHTING 74
5. FIGHTING 84
6. FIGHTING 96
7. FIGHTING 92 — SILVER KINGS
8. GRIM REAPERS — VF-101
9. VF-102 DIAMONDBACKS

1

2

3

4

5

6

7

8

9

1. ONE TWENTY FOUR
2. VF 124 GUNFIGHTERS
3. VF 124 GUNFIGHTERS
4. VF-126 BANDITS — THE BAD GUYS
5. PACIFIC FLEET ADVERSARY — STRKFITRON 127
6. FIGHTING 131
7.
8. GHOSTRIDERS
9. SANS REPROACHE — FIGHTING 143

Fighter Squadrons

Fighter Squadrons

1. VF-194 Red Lightning
(Hellfires)

2. VF-201 Hunters

3. VF-202 Superheats

4. VF-202 Superheats

5. VF-202 Superheats

6. VF-211 Fighting Checkmates

7. VF-213 Black Lions

Fighter Squadrons

- 1. VF-301 Devil's Disciples (R)
- 2. VF-301 Devil's Disciples (L)
- 3. VF-302 Stallions

- 4. VF-1285 Fighting Fujibars
- 5. VF-1285 NAS Miramar
- 6. U.S. Naval Aviation Aviator

- 7. VF-1485 The Americans
- 8. U.S. Naval Aviation Air Crew

Attack
Squadrons

Attack
Squadrons

Attack Squadrons

■ 1. VA-12 Clinchers

■ 2. VA-12 Clinchers

■ 3. VA-22 Fighting Redcocks

■ 4. VA-22 Fighting Redcocks

■ 5. Attack Squadron 23

■ 6. VA-34 Blue Blasters

■ 7. VA-34 Blue Blasters

■ 8. VA-35 Black Panthers On Board USS Constellation

1

2

3

4

5

6

7

8

9

Attack Squadrons

1. VA-35 Black Panthers

2. VA-36 Roadrunners

3. VA-37 Bulls

4. VA-37 Bulls Special
Weapons Team

5. VA-56 Champions

6. VA-42 Green Pawns

7. VA-42 Green Pawns
Safety Award

8. VA-42 Green Pawns
Maintenance

1

2

3

4

5

6

7

8

9

1

2

3

4

5

6

7

8

10

9

1

2

3

4

5

6

7

8

9

1

2

3

4

5

6

7

8

9

1

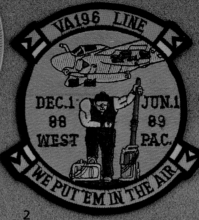

2

3

4

5

6

7

8

1

3

2

4

5

6

7

Fighter-Attack
Squadrons

Fighter-Attack Squadrons

Ten examples of patches made specifically for the F/A 18 Hornet. The large centerpiece was made for the back of a flight jacket or "Party Jacket".

- 1.
- 2.
- 3.
- 4.
- 5.
- 6.
- 7.
- 8.
- 9.
- 10.

Fighter-Attack Squadrons

1. STRKFITRON-15

2. VFA-25 Fist of the Fleet

3. VFA-25 Fist of the Fleet

4. VFA-82 F/A 18 Patch

5. VFA-81 Sunliners

6. VFA-86 F/A 18C Sidewinders

7. STRKFITRON-82 Marauders

8. STRKFITRON-86 Sidewinders

9. VFA-106 Gladiators

10. VFA-106 Gladiators

Fighter-Attack Squadrons

1. VFA-113 Stingers

2. VFA-113 Stingers

3. STRKFITRON-125 Rough Raiders

4. VFA-125 NAS Fallon

5. VFA-131 Wildcats

6. VFA-131 Wildcats

7. VFA-132 Privateers

8. VFA-132 Privateers

9. VFA-132 Privateers

1

2

3

4

5

6

7

8

Fighter-Attack Squadrons

■ 1. VFA-195 Dambusters

■ 2. VFA-195 Dambusters

■ 3.VFA-195 Dambusters

1

2

3

4

5

6

7

8

9

Fighter-Attack Squadrons

1. STRKFITRON-303
   Golden Hawks

2. VFA-303 F/A-18 Hornet

3. VFA-305 Lobos

4. Attack Squadron-305 Lobos

5. Attack Squadron-305 Lobos

6. Attack Squadron-305 Lobos

7. McDonnell Douglas
   F/A-18 Hornet

8. McDonnell Douglas
   F/A-18 Hornet

F-14 Tomcat
Patches

Tomcat Patches

Here are illustrated various examples of the same design executed by several different manufacturers. The example in the center is designed to be worn on the back of a flight jacket or "Party Jacket". The smaller designs are from flight clothing.

1.

2.

3.

4.

5.

6.

7.

8.

9.

Tomcat Squadrons

1. Ground Crew and Maintenance

2. Flight Test Crew

3. C.D.I.

Three examples of "Front Seat" designs.

4.

5.

6.

Grumman designs for delivery of F-14s to; (7) Japan, (8) Iran and (9) Iran ("Tomcat" in Arabic). They were designed but never used except for (9) Iran, which accompanied the delivery of 80 F-14 to the Shah of Iran before the takeover.

7.   8.   9.

Tomcat Squadrons

Examples of Tomcat designs used by various squadrons equipped with F-14 aircraft.

- 1. VF-1 Wolfpack

- 2. VF-2 Bountyhunters

- 3. VF-11 Red Rippers

- 4. VF-14 Tophatters

- 5. VF-14 Tophatters

- 6. VF-21 Freelancers

- 7. VF-31 Tomcatters

- 8. VF-31 Tomcatters

- 9. VF-32 Swordsmen

1

2

3

4

5

6

7

8

9

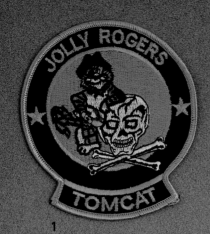

1

2

3

4

5

6

7

8

9

1

2

3

4

5

6

7

8

9

1

2

3

4

5

6

7

8

9

Tomcat Squadrons

1. VF-154 Black Knights

2. VF-154 Black Knights

3. VF-154 Black Knights

4. VF-194 Red Lightnings

5. VF-201 Hunters

6. VF-202 Superheats

7. VF-201 Hunters

8. VF-202 Superheats

9. VF-211 Checkmates

Tomcat Squadrons

Tomcat Squadrons

1. VF-2 Bountyhunters

2. VF-14 Tophatters

3. VF-32 Swordsmen

4. VF-154 Black Knights

5. TARPS Generic

6. TARPS Generic

7. Television Surveillance Unit

8. VF-32 Swordsmen
   Lebanon-1986

9. Tweakers • Maintenance Crew

F-14D Super Tomcat and Libyan
Action Units.

Three different examples of designs produced after the Libyan
action of April, 1986.

1. F-14D Super Tomcat

4. F-14A+ Advanced
   Model Aircraft

7.

2. F-14D Super Tomcat

5. Libyan action • 1986 • 4 for 4

8.

3. F-14D Super Tomcat

6. CV-67 Mig Buster • Libya 1986

9.

Tomcat Patches

100, 200 and 300 times indicate the number of carrier arrested landings successfully completed in an F-14.

"ANYTIME, BABY" Novelty companions to the original Tomcat patches. The large center example was made for either a flight jacket or the ever-popular "Party Jacket". An example

in French also exists which was made for the Paris Air Show.

"100 DARK ONES, BABY" refers to night carrier arrested landings sucessfully completed in an F-14.

◼ 1.

◼ 2.

◼ 3.

◼ 4.

◼ 5.

◼ 6.

◼ 7.

◼ 8.

◼ 9.

Tomcat Cruises

☐ 1. USS Nimitz Westpac-88

☐ 2. USS Nimitz Westpac-88-89

☐ 3. USS Nimitz Westpac-89

☐ 4. USS America Perth 1987

☐ 5. USS Enterprise Perth 1986

☐ 6. USS Constellation Perth 1988

☐ 7. F-14 Tomcat

☐ 8. F-14 Tomcat
Imperial Iranian Air Force

☐ 9. F-14 Tomcat
The Cats Night Out

Tomcat Triangles

1. VF-31 Tomcatters

2. "He is my preferred toy" Novelty Jacket Patch

3. VF-101 Grim Reapers

4. VF-301 Devils Disciples

5. VF-194 Hellfires

6. Subdued Version

7. VF-202 Superheats

1

2

3

4

5

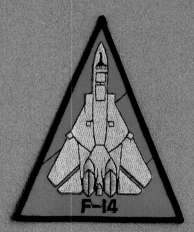

6

Tomcat Triangles

■ 1. VF-1 Wolfpack

■ 2. VF-1 Wolfpack

■ 3. VF-2 Bounty Hunters

■ 5. Nameplates for Aviator's
Flight Bag

■ 6. Nameplates for VF-51
Screaming Eagles

■ 8. VF-213 Black Lions

■ 9. VF-24 Renegades

1

2

3

4

5

6

7

8

9

1

2

VF-102

3

VF-103

4

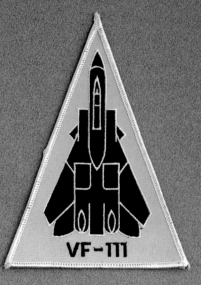

VF-111

5

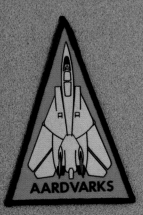

AARDVARKS

6

VF-154

7

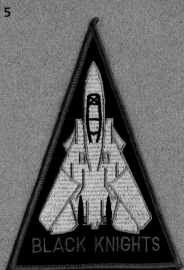

BLACK KNIGHTS

8

Blue Angels

The patches shown on this page and the following page were worn by members of the Blue Angels, the Navy's crack aerial demonstration team. The designs illustrate the various types of aircraft used by the team throughout its colorful history.

■ 1.

■ 2.

■ 3.

■ 4.

■ 5.

■ 6.

■ 7.

■ 8.

■ 9.

1

2

3

4

5

6

7

8

US Navy Fighter Weapons School

"Top Gun" and Aggressor Squadrons

US Navy Fighter Weapons School "Top Gun" and Aggressors

1. USNFWS Aggressor

2. USNFWS Cap Patch

3. USNFWS Aggressor

4. USNFWS (small)

5. USNFWS

6. "Top Gun" Movie Logo

7. "Top Gun" Movie Logo

8. "Top Gun" Movie Logo

9. "Top Gun" Movie Logo

10. "Top Gun" Movie Logo

USN and USMC Aggressor Units

1. Nameplate for Aggressor Pilot

2. Aggressor Squadron 12

3. VF-43 Challengers Triangle

4. Nameplate for Aggressor Pilot

5. Nameplate for Aggressor Pilot

6. Road Gang

7. VF-43 Challengers Triangle

8. FITRON-43

1

2

3

4

5

6

7

8

Tactical Electronic Squadrons

Fleet Air Reconnaissance Squadrons

Anti-Submarine Squadrons

Tactical Electronic Squadrons

- 1. VAQ-33 Firebirds
- 2. VAQ-34 Aggressors
- 3. VAQ-34 Electric Horsemen
- 4. VAQ-129 Vikings

- 5. VAQ-129 Vikings
- 6. VAQ-130 Zappers
- 7. VAQ-130 Zappers
- 8. VAQ-131 Lancers

- 9. VAQ-131 Lancers
- 10. VAQ-131 Lancers

Tactical Electronic Squadrons

1. VAQ-132 Scorpions

2. VAQ-133 Wizards

3. VAQ-133 Wizards

4. VAQ-134 Garudas

5. VAQ-136 Gauntlets

6. VAQ-136 Gauntlets

7. VAQ-137 Cap Patch

8. TACELRON-138 (small)

9. VAQ-137 Rooks

10. VAQ-138 Yellow Jackets

11. TACELRON-138
Yellow Jackets

1

2

3

4

5

6

7

8

9

Anti-Submarine Squadrons

- 1. AIRANTISUBRON-21 Fighting Redtails
- 2. AIRANTISUBRON-21 Fighting Redtails
- 3. VS-22 Checkmates
- 4. VS-22 Checkmates
- 5. AIRANTISUBRON-24 Scouts
- 6. VS-24 Scouts Mediterranean Cruise
- 7. VS-27
- 8. VS-28 Gamblers
- 9. AIRASRON-28 Gamblers

Anti-Submarine Squadrons

- 1. VS-30 Diamond Cutters

- 2. AIRASRON-31 Top Cats

- 3. VS-32 Maulers

- 5. VS-33 World Famous
  Screwbirds

- 6. VS-33 World Famous
  Screwbirds

- 8. AIRANTISUBRON-41

- 9. VS-892

Carrier Early Warning Squadrons

Fleet Composite Squadrons

Photographic Squadrons

Carrier Airborne Early Warning
Squadrons

1. VAW-78 Fighting Escargots

2. CARAEWRON-88 Cottonpickers

3. VAW-110

4. VAW-111 Hawks

5. VAW-112 Golden Hawks

6. VAW-112 Golden Hawks

7. VAW-113 Black Eagles

8. VAW-114 Hormel Hawgs

9. VAW-114 Hormel Hawgs

Carrier Airborne Early Warning
Squadrons

1. VAW-116 Sun Kings

2. VAW-117 Nighthawks

3. VAW-120 Greyhawks

4. VAW-120 Greyhawks

5. VAW-121 Bluetails

6. VA-122

7. VAW-122 Steel Jaw

8. VAW-123 Screwtop

Carrier Airborne Early Warning Squadrons, Composite Squadrons and Photographic squadrons

■ 1. VAW-124 Bear Aces

■ 2. VAW-126 Seahawks

■ 3. VAW-127 Seabats

■ 4. VAW-1086 Augger Dogger

■ 5. VC-13 Saints

■ 6. VCS-2

■ 7. VC-76

■ 8. VFP-63 Eyes of the Fleet

■ 9. VFP-206 Hawkeyes

**Patrol
Squadrons**

**Transport and
Support
Squadrons**

**Training
Squadrons**

**Training Aircraft
Types**

Patrol Squadrons

- 1. Patrol Unit II

- 2. PATRON-6 Blue Sharks

- 3. PATRON-8

- 4. PATRON-8

- 5. Patrol Squadron-8

- 6. VP-11 Pegasus

- 7. VP-11 Pegasus

- 8. VP-16 Eagles

1

2

3

4

5

6

7

8

Patrol Squadrons

- 1. VP-46 Grey Knights
  Maintenence

- 2. VP-46 Grey Knights

- 3. PATRON-50 Blue Dragons

- 4. PATRON-56 Dragons

- 5. VP-60 Cobras

- 6. PATRON-62 Broadarrows

- 7. VP-64 Condors

- 8. VP-64 Ordnance

Patrol Squadrons

- 1. PATRON-66

- 2. PATRON-91 Stingers

- 3. PATRON-92 Minutemen

- 4. PATRON-93 Executioners

- 5. PATRON-94 Crawfishers

- 6. VAP-62

- 7. VFP-206 Hawkeyes

- 8. Patrol Bombing Squadron-15

Transport and Support Squadrons

1 SAUFLEY'S VT-1 SATANS

2 TRARON ONE

3 TRAINING SQUADRON TWO

4 VT-3

5 VT-IV

6 VT-4

7 TRAINING SQUADRON SEVEN

8

9 WORLDS GREATEST TRAINING SQUADRON — TRAINING SQUADRON SIX

10 TRAINING SQUADRON SEVEN

Training Squadrons

- 1. TRARON-3 Red Max

- 2. TRARON-3 Red Knights

- 3. TRARON-86

- 5. HELTRARON-18

- 6. TA-4 F-18 Instructor

- 7. TA-4 T-34 Instructor

- 8. F-18 Instructor with 500 combat-free hours

- 9. T-34 Instructor with 500 combat-free hours

Training Squadrons

Training Squadrons

- 1. VT-24 Bobcats
- 2. TRARON-26
- 3. VT-27-II Neuces' Aces

- 4. TRARON-27 Boomers
- 5. TRARON-27 Boomers
- 6. TRARON-28

- 7. VT-28 Rangers
- 8. TRARON-29
- 9. VT-31

1

2

3

4

5

6

7

8

9

Aircraft Carrier Air Wings

Combat Aircrews

Unusual Stations

Carrier Air Wings

- 1. CVW-1
- 2. CVW-2
- 3. CVW-3
- 4. CVW-5
- 5. CVW-6
- 6. CVW-7
- 7. CVW-8
- 8. CVW-9

CARRIER AIR WING 10

CVW 11

AIR WING 13 GUARDIANS

CVW FORTUNA FAVET FORTIBUS 1A

CARRIER AIR WING 16

CVW 17

FLEET AIR WING

Combat Aircrews

- 1. Combat Aircrew-2

- 2. Combat Aircrew-3

- 3. Combat Aircrew-11 Warpigs

- 4. Combat Aircrew-5
  Freedom Fighters

- 5. Keflavik 1986

- 6. Combat Aircrew-10

- 7. Combat Aircrew-4 Rondel's
  Flying Circus

- 8. Combat Aircrew-12 Vipers

Combat Aircrews and Unusual Stations

1. Combat Aircrew-9 Iceland 1989

2. Combat Aircrew-2

3. ANTARCTIDEVRON-6
Puckered Penguins

4. Combat Aircrew-6
Rota-Lajes-1988

5. Andros Ranges - AUTEC

6. Naval Facility - Adak, Alaska

7. Naval Facility - Keflavik, Iceland

Centurion,
Carrier Landing
Patches

Efficiency
and Safety
Awards

Centurions

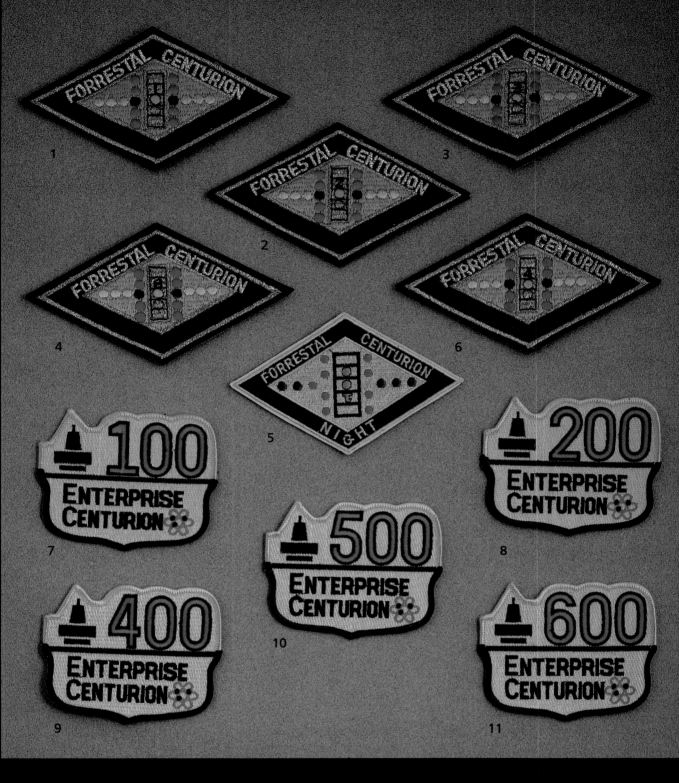

Centurions

1

2

3

4

5

6

7

8

9

1

3

2

4

6

5

7

8

9

10

1

2

3

4

5

6

7

8

Centurions

1. USS Coral Sea 100

2. USS Coral Sea 200

3. USS Coral Sea 300

5. USS Coral Sea Top Ten

6. Tailhook Association (unofficial)

7. Tailhook Association

8. Tailhook Association Aviator with 100 Arrested Landings

9. Tailhook Association Air Crew

Centurions

Carrier Landing Patches

1. Landing Ship Officer

2. Plat Landing Ship Officer

3. Landing Ship Officer School

4. 100 Carrier Landings

5. S-3 Viking Tailhook Senso

6. AIRLANT Landing Ship Officer

7. 100 Air Operations Meetings

8. 100 A-4 Skyhawk Landings

9. 300 Hawkeye Traps

1

2

3

NAVAL AIR FORCE
COMMANDER
ATLANTIC FLEET
E
BATTLE EFFICIENCY
USS SARATOGA CV-60
1986

NAVAL AIR FORCE
COMMANDER
ATLANTIC FLEET
E
VP-16
1983

NAVAL AIR FORCE
COMMANDER
ATLANTIC FLEET
E
BATTLE EFFICIENCY
VA-81
1987

4

AVIATION SAFETY AWARD
1983
CNO
VA-97

5

NORTH ATLANTIC
88
V F
8 4
E
#

7

1986-87
AIRPAC
WINNERS
VFA 25

6

VF142

Aircraft Carriers

1

2

3

PLANK OWNER

4

CABOT ★ CVL 28

U.S.S. WASP

U.S.S. PRINCETON

5

6

7

U.S.S. SHANGRI-LA

CVA-43

CVA-43

8

9

10

Aircraft Carriers

■ 1. USS Valley Forge CV-45

■ 2. Carrier Aviation (novelty)

■ 3. USS Franklin CV-13

■ 4. Plank Owner

■ 5. USS Cabot CVL-28

■ 6. USS Wasp CV-7

■ 7. USS Princeton CVS-37

■ 8. USS Shangri-La CVS-38

■ 9. USS Coral Sea CV-43

■ 10. USS Coral Sea CVA-43
(Menorah Mast)

1

2

3

4

5

6

7

8

Aircraft Carriers

- 1. USS Palau CVE-122
- 2. USS Ranger CV-61
- 3. USS Ranger CV-61
- 4. USS Ranger CV-61
- 5. USS Kitty Hawk CV-63
- 6. USS Constellation CV-64
- 7. USS Enterprise CVN-65
- 8. USS America CV-66
  Libya-1986

U.S. Marine
Corps Aviation

Marine Corps Aviation

■ 1. VMF (AW)-114

■ 2. VMF-212 Devilcats

■ 3. VMF-124

■ 4. VMF-214 Blacksheep

■ 5. VMF-214 Blacksheep

■ 6. VMF-214 "A" Shift

■ 7. VMF-222 Flying Dueces

■ 8. VMF-222

1

2

3

4

5

6

7

8

Marine Corps Aviation

Marine Corps Aviation

1. VMFA-314 Black Knights

2. VMFA-314 Black Knights

3. VMFA-314 Black Knights

4. VMFA-321 Hell's Angels

5. VMFA-321 Hell's Angels

6. VMFA-323 Death Rattlers

7. VMFA-323 Death Rattlers

8. VMFA-333 Shamrocks

9. VMFA-333 Shamrocks

Marine Corps Aviation

1. VMFA-451 Warlords (large)
2. VMFA-451 Warlords F-18
3. VMFA-451 Warlords F-4

4. VMFA-513 Flying Nightmares
5. VMF (N)-531 Grey Ghosts
6. VMFA-531 Grey Ghosts

7. HMX-1 Executive Detachment
8. HMX-1 Executive Detachment
9. HMX-1 Executive Detachment

1

2

3

4

5

6

7

8

9

1

2

3

4

5

6

7

8

9

1

2

3

4

5

6

7

8

9

1 VMA-542

2 PROWLER VMAQ-2

3 CAN DO EASY VMAQ-2

4 VMAQ-2

5 SEAHAWKS VMAQ-4

6 VMO-1

7 3RD MARINE DIVISION AIR OBSERVER SECTION VMO-2

8 EVIL EYES VMO-4

9 VMO-4

11

Marine Corps Aviation

- 1. VMAT-102
- 2. VMT-203
- 3. VMAT (AW)-202 Twilight Tour

- 4. MAWTS-1
- 5. VMC-2
- 6. VMGR-152

- 7. VMGR-252
- 8. VMGR-352 Raiders
- 9. VMGR-352

Glossary

System Of Aircraft Identification Numbers and Names

In 1962, the Department Of Defense ordered that all military services standardize the aircraft numbering system. This was intended to end the confusion that had existed for several years due to each branch of service designing their own aircraft numbering system. For instance, the Army's, B-25D would also be the Navy's PBJ-1D.

This new system had been in place for some years and had been earlier adopted by the Air Force. To avoid further confusion for the Navy, their aircraft were marked with both systems for the next year. Under the new Department Of Defense system, an aircraft designation may consist of up to four elements:

Mission/Type Modification Symbol	Basic Mission\Type Symbol	Aircraft Series Number	Model Series Letter
E	A	6	B

Mission\Type Modification Symbol:

These are prefix letters, indicating an aircraft modified for other than its original basic mission.

Letter	Meaning
A	Attack
C	Cargo\Transport
D	Drone Control
E	Special Electronics
H	Search & Rescue
K	Tanker
L	Cold Weather Operations
M	Missle Capability
O	Observation
Q	Drone
R	Reconnaissance
S	Anti-Submarine
T	Trainer
U	Utility
V	Staff Transport
W	Weather Reconnaissance

Basic Mission\Type Symbol:

These are to indicate an aircraft's primary mission. However, some (e.g., Z) indicate its type. Letter symbols indicating mission modification (above) or special status (below) are prefixed to this basic symbol.

Letter	Meaning
A	Attack
B	Bomber
C	Cargo\Transport
E	Special Electronics
F	Fighter
H	Helicopter
K	Tanker
O	Observation
P	Patrol
S	Anti-Submarine
T	Trainer
U	Utility
V	Vertical Take-off and Landing (VTOL & STOL)
X	Research
Z	Airship

Aircraft Series Number:

These numbers are assigned sequentially within each basic mission category regardless of designer or manufacturer. This is basically the same system used by the Army and the Air Force since 1919. The number is separated from the basic mission symbol by a dash.

Model Series Letter:

This letter, when added to the series number, indicates an improvement or alteration of the basic model. These are assigned in sequence, i.e. F-14A; F-14B; F-14C, etc.

Status Prefix Symbol:

This letter symbol, which is not a part of the normal designation, indicates prototype and experimental or other special status:

Letter	Meaning
G	Permanently grounded
J	Special test - temporary
N	Special test - permanent
X	Experimental
Y	Prototype
Z	Planning

Nicknames:

Initiated during World War II and continuing until today, nicknames for aircraft have been recognized by the Navy. Ever since the war years every Navy airplane has been referred to by its type designation and also by an offically approved nickname.

Type Designation	Nickname
F\A-18	Hornet
F-14	Tomcat
A-6E	Intruder
A-7E	Corsair
EA-6B	Prowler
E6-A	Tacamo

E-2C	Hawkeye
P-3C	Orion
S-3A	Viking
C-130	Hercules
C-2A	Greyhound
C-9B	Skytrain II
T-45A	Goshawk

Unit Indicators:

Each aviation unit has an alphanumerical designation which will indicate information regarding the unit:

Style of Aircraft	Navy or Marine Corps	Mission Of Unit	Numerical Designation
V	M	F	124

Style Of Aircraft:

Indicates whether the aircraft is:

V	Heavier than air
H	Helicopter
Z	Lighter than air

Navy or Marine Corps:

Indicates whether the unit is a part of the:

Navy = No letter, or
U.S. Marine Corps = M

Mission of unit:

Indicates the unit's primary mission:

A	Attack
AQ	Electronics

AW	Early Warning
C	Cargo
F	Fighter
FA	Fighter Attack
H	Helicopter
O	Composite
P	Patrol
Q	Electronics
R	Transport
S	Anti-submarine
T	Training
X	Experimental or Executive

Index

Bibliography

If you are interested in the hobby of collecting Naval Aviation patches, perhaps this book will act as a guide for the systematic accumulation of the designs pictured herein. We have provided a space for you to indicate when you have collected a particular item. We will plan to do this also in future volumes.

I realize that much more is to be done in bringing to light the myriad of insignia that have been used through the years. To this end, I ask your help in making these designs available for future use. If you would care to contribute to the store of knowledge on the subject, please make available to the publisher any designs or emblems that are not pictured here. We will publish them in future volumes as they become available with acknowledgement to you for your contribution.

American Society of Military Insignia Collectors, "The Trading Post", Midlothian, VA . Published Quarterly

Doll, T. E., Jackson, B.R. & Riley, W. A, *Navy Air Colors,* Squadron/Signal Publications, 1985, Carrollton, TX

Gervasi, Tom, *Arsenal of Democracy,* Grove Press, 1981, New York, NY

Hubbard, G., *"Aircraft Insignia, Spirit of Youth,"* National Geographic Magazine, June 1943, Washington, DC

Kasulka, Duane, *USN Aircraft Carrier Air Units, Vol. 3,* Squadron/Signal publications, 1988, Carrollton, TX

Kinzey, Bert, *F-14A & B Tomcat,* Tab Books, 1982, Blue Ridge Summit, PA

Kinzey, Bert, & Leader, Ray, *Colors and Markings of the F-14 Tomcat,* Tab Books, 1987, Blue Ridge Summit, PA

Koku-Fan, No. 5, Periodical, Published monthly in Japan, May 1986

Lawson, R.L., Editor, *The History of US Naval Air Power,* The Military Press, 1987, New York, NY

Peacock, L., *F-14 Tomcat Squadrons of the US Navy,* Ian Allen, Ltd., 1986, Runnymede, England

Polmar, N., *World Combat Aircraft Directory,* Doubleday, 1976, New York, NY

The Tailhook Association, "The Hook, Journal of Carrier Aviation," Bonita, CA. Published Quarterly.

U.S. Navy, *Dictionary of American Naval Fighting Ships,* U.S. Government Printing Office, 1979, Washington, DC